HOW TO MASTER SCHOOL

By Brooks Whitney

Previously published as *How to Master the School Universe: Homework, Teachers, Tests, Bullies, and Other Ways to Survive the Classroom*, 2004.

SCHOLASTIC INC.

New York Toronto London Auckland Sydney
Mexico City New Delhi Hong Kong Buenos Aires

The recommendations and advice included in this book are based on research and expert information. The publisher and author have made every effort to ensure that the information presented is complete and accurate. The publisher, author, and illustrator disclaim any liability that may result from the use of the information in this book.

ISBN: 0-439-89978-8

Design: Joe Borzetta
Illustrations: Kelly Kennedy

Copyright © 2004 by Scholastic Inc.

All rights reserved. Published by Scholastic Inc.

Previously published as *How to Master the School Universe: Homework, Teachers, Tests, Bullies, and Other Ways to Survive the Classroom*, 2004.

Revised edition © 2006

SCHOLASTIC, HOW TO MASTER EVERYTHING CLUB, and associated logos are trademarks and/or registered trademarks of Scholastic Inc.

12 11 10 9 8 7 6 5 4 3 2 1   6 7 8 9 10 11/0

Printed in China   First Scholastic printing, October 2006

Contents

Master It!

Do you like school, or do you kind of dread it? Maybe you liked school last week, but this week it's no fun at all. No matter what kind of student you are, or what grades you get, some of the time you probably feel like you need help.

Maybe you worry about your grades and how you can do better. Maybe you're more focused on your social life, getting a part in a play, or making the soccer team. Whatever you've been thinking about, this book is packed full of strategies and tips to help you get from where you are right now to where you want to be.

If you use the ideas you find in this book, you can make everything about school easier and more fun. Even days when you have a test or tons of homework can be made manageable with a few simple tricks.

You'll read about ways to organize yourself and your time, and how better organization can lead to better grades—without extra studying! You'll learn to master a variety of classroom situations, including testy teachers, group projects, and embarrassing moments.

You'll also discover some really important information about a super important topic—you! Do you know how you, as an individual, learn best? Knowing your own learning style can help you study faster and make all the stuff you've studied stick. But what if you draw a total blank on test day and have nothing in your mind but fear? Read on and you'll find solutions to just that kind of testing situation.

Of course, school's not just about what happens in the classroom. You'll find tips for dealing with all sorts of after-school situations—from confrontations with bullies, to not getting picked for class president, from starting your own club, to getting your homework done on time. These are all aspects of school that you can master.

YOU CAN DO IT!

Read this guide straight through from cover to cover, or skip from section to section based on what worries or interests you most. Mastering school and getting more of what you want—and less of what you don't want!—is within your reach. It all starts, right now, with you—and your student style.

WHAT'S YOUR STUDENT STYLE?

Do you try your hardest to do well in school, or do you just slip by? Read the questions below and circle the answers that describe you best. Be honest!

1. Your teacher assigns a big history report that's due in three weeks. With so much time, you figure you can wait a week or two before starting and still have plenty of time to get it done.
  a. Yep, that's me
  b. Sometimes that's me
  c. I wouldn't do that

2. When working on your history report, you figure you can save time with a one-stop shop and get all your info out of an encyclopedia.
  a. Yep, that's me
  b. Sometimes that's me
  c. I wouldn't do that

3. When taking a test, you decide it's a waste of time to do a quick review to see what's ahead and to identify trouble spots. Instead, you start at the beginning and work problem by problem.

  a. Yep, that's me
  b. Sometimes that's me
  c. I wouldn't do that

4. During the test, you get stuck on the essay question. Even though it's taking much more time than you'd expected, and you know you'd be better at the multiple-choice questions, you stick with it.
  a. Yep, that's me
  b. Sometimes that's me
  c. I wouldn't do that

5. Your favorite movie is on TV, but you still have a lot of reading to do. You decide to compromise and do your reading—but have the TV on in the background.
  a. Yep, that's me
  b. Sometimes that's me
  c. I wouldn't do that

6. You sit down to do your reading and realize that your pen has dried up. No big deal. You decide that you don't really need it anyway because you're sure to remember the important stuff.
  a. Yep, that's me
  b. Sometimes that's me
  c. I wouldn't do that

7. Your best friend is begging you to let him cheat off you during the spelling test. You agree to let him do it—you figure, just this once!

    a. Yep, that's me

    b. Sometimes that's me

    c. I wouldn't do that

8. Even though you're on the soccer team, play in the jazz band, and take trumpet lessons after school, you decide to try out for the school play, too. If you can't get your homework done before bed, you can always do it on the bus in the morning.

    a. Yep, that's me

    b. Sometimes that's me

    c. I wouldn't do that

9. When you get a test or assignment back with a not-so-great grade, you throw it in your book bag without a second thought.

    a. Yep, that's me

    b. Sometimes that's me

    c. I wouldn't do that

10. Your teacher is showing the class a math problem at the board and it seems like everyone in the class "gets it" but you. You decide to keep quiet and figure out the math problem by yourself later.

    a. Yep, that's me

    b. Sometimes that's me

    c. I wouldn't do that

REPORT CARD

Give yourself two points for every *c* you circled, and one point for every *b*. Give yourself zero points for every *a*.

Super Student (14–20 points) From good time management, to smart study strategies, your actions show that you take school seriously. Your smart school sense is sure to bring success. Read this book to get tips on how to polish your A+ skills even further!

Satisfactory Student (8–13 points) There's still room for improvement. A little more effort on your part could help you get better grades! Read on and make sure to note the sections that you're still struggling with.

S.O.S.—Save Our Student! (0–7 points) It looks like you need some help! No worries—read on for some super strategies to help you make the grade!

First, Master Yourself

Y ou can help yourself do better in school before you even walk through the door! No books, no teachers, no studying—just a little time spent getting yourself organized. Are you drowning under piles of old papers and dried-up pens? Do you have too much to do and not enough time to do it? Read on to find out why getting it together at home can make a big difference in how you do in school!

GET READY!

Whether it's the beginning of the school year, somewhere in the middle, or almost the end, it's never too late to make a fresh start. From organizing your study space at home to getting the school supplies you need, a few simple preparations will help you a lot!

Trash It!

De-junking will unclutter your brain. Clean out your backpack, old folders, and desk drawers. Trash stuff that no longer works or serves a purpose, like dried-up pens, pencil stubs, worn-out erasers, crusty whiteout, and candy wrappers.

Store It!

Keep any old papers, reports, or tests you want to save in a pocket folder. On the front of the folder write down what's inside.

Space Place

All students need a good study space—a special spot where your mind clicks into study mode when you sit down. When choosing your space, make sure it has:

1. Quiet. Pick a place that isn't near a TV or in the center of everything else happening at home.

2. Good light, so you don't strain your eyes. Natural light from a window is considered best, but a bright lamp works great, too. And you'll need that at night, anyway.

3. A flat surface, like a desk or table, to write on.

4. A straight-backed chair. It should be comfortable, but not so comfy that you fall asleep!

SCHOOL TOOLS

Doctors, dentists, architects, construction workers, chefs, and other professionals all have special tools to help them succeed at their jobs. Make a list of the supplies you'll need to get your job done. Here's an example:

paper

pencils and erasers, pens, markers

pencil sharpener

assignment book

folders

notebooks

binders

dictionary

sticky notes

stapler and staples

tape

scissors

ruler

computer

calendar or date book

Bright Idea

Places, Please!

Once you've de-junked, get organized. Use everyday household items to clean up your clutter and organize your study space.

Silverware Divider: You're used to seeing these inside kitchen drawers, keeping silverware organized, but they work great for organizing school supplies, too. Put markers in one space, colored pencils in another, your ruler in the next, and so on. Either slip the divider into your desk drawer, or keep it on the table within easy reach while you're doing your homework.

Junior Jars: Small jars, like those used for baby food, are perfect for storing paper clips, staples, spare change, and other small stuff you want to keep track of. And they fit neatly into a drawer! To remove the label, soak the empty jar in hot, soapy water until it comes off. Use a sponge to scrub off any sticky stuff.

Box It: Store extra paper, magazines, and school handouts in recycled cereal boxes. When the cereal is gone, throw out the inside bag and cut off the top flaps. Cut the box diagonally on both sides. Decorate with wrapping paper or make a collage by gluing on pictures cut out of magazines.

Pocket Stuffers: Hanging shoe holders have lots of pockets for storing lots of stuff—other than shoes! From paints and paint brushes, to stationery, notepads, rolls of tape, and jars of glue, there's a place for everything. Hang the shoe holder in your closet to keep it out of the way.

GET SET!

Now that your stuff is organized, do you yourself have it together? Taking care of yourself may not seem like it has much to do with how you do in school, but it does! Read on for a few simple tips that will help you feel great throughout the Monday-Friday day.

Get a Good Night's Sleep

When you're tired, it means your brain is tired, too. Having a tired brain makes for a very long school day! It's harder to pay attention, think smart, and participate. You're more likely to space out, yawn loudly while the teacher's talking, and stare at the clock for long periods of time. To combat sleepy-student syndrome, get eight hours of sleep a night. Being well rested will help you stay sharp!

Eat a Healthful Breakfast

Studies show that kids who eat breakfast do better in school. It makes sense—who can concentrate on math problems and geography tests with a rumbling stomach and a brain filled with thoughts of lunch? Food is fuel. Use it to power your body and brain before you head out the door. And if you bag your lunch, don't forget to take it with you!

Bright Idea

Brainy Breakfasts

Try these quickie breakfasts that you can grab on the go!

Sunrise Smoothies

Mix a glass of orange juice, half a container of vanilla yogurt, a banana chopped into pieces, and four ice cubes in a blender. Blend on high until everything is mixed up and frothy. Slurp on your way to school!

Scoop It Up!

Mix up a batch of this crunchy morning meal on wheels. Scoop into a resealable plastic bag, grab a carton of juice or milk, and go!

Add 1 cup of all these ingredients together and shake well.
- mixed nuts like almonds, cashews, pistachios, and pecans
- raisins or dried cranberries
- yogurt-covered raisins or nuts
- granola, oat, or rice cereal (or any of your other faves)
- shredded coconut

P, B & J Waffle-wich

Toast two frozen waffles, then spread with peanut butter and jelly. Put them together to make a sandwich.

It's a Wrap!

To make this breakfast burrito, roll up your favorite ingredients in a tortilla and microwave (with a grown-up's help) for 20 seconds, until it's all gooey and good! Here are a few to try:
- cream cheese & jelly • peanut butter & banana
- sliced apple and raisins drizzled with honey

Pizza Bagels for Breakfast!

Toast a bagel, then spread each half with ketchup or tomato sauce and top with a slice of cheese. Pop the bagel, open face, in the toaster oven until the cheese melts.

Put Yourself Together

Being put together isn't about wearing the latest styles or having the biggest wardrobe. It's simply about taking the time to put yourself together! What does your appearance say about you? Do you look like you just rolled out of bed, or are you neat and tidy, ready to master the school universe instead? Just like your folks put themselves together for work, you should do the same for school. And just like being in your pajamas helps you get ready for sleep, putting yourself together will help your mind click into school mode.

You can also help get your mind into school mode by packing your backpack with care. Before you begin, take everything out of your bag so you know what's in there. Then put back only what you need. (So, if you don't have math on Thursdays, don't carry your math book with you on that day.) Put each book and notebook in your bag in the order that you will use it, keeping your books for your first class in the front and those for the end of the day at the back. When you get to class, you'll have an easy time pulling out the right stuff, instead of fumbling around for the things you need. Use the outside pockets on your bag for pens, pencils, and erasers. That way you can find them quickly, too.

Go!

An airplane pilot goes through a series of checks before takeoff, and so should you! From homework assignments to the right folder and books, you can do better in school by simply not forgetting important stuff! It only takes a couple of minutes to make sure you have everything you need.

CHECK ✔ POINT

Before Taking Off For School

Make sure you have:

- ✓ books
- ✓ plenty of paper, your notebooks, sharpened pencils, and a few pens
- ✓ finished homework
- ✓ lunch or lunch money
- ✓ signed permission slips
- ✓ house keys
- ✓ gym clothes

Master the Classroom

Most of what you learn takes place in the classroom. So it's smart to know how to listen and how to take notes. Your attitude counts for something, too. Teachers are impressed by students who try! Think about it: Do you participate in class discussion? Sit where you can see the board? Keep quiet when your teacher is speaking? These are all things that can affect your grade. Keep reading to learn how to make the most of class time!

Ten Ways to Do Better in Class without Even Cracking a Book

1. Make sure you have everything you need before class starts.

2. Be on time.

3. Write down all your assignments so you don't forget anything.

4. Turn things in when you're supposed to.

5. Speak up! Taking part in class discussions can improve your grade.

6. Don't talk while your teacher's talking.

7. Ask questions if you don't understand.

8. Take the time to go over assignments and tests before turning them in.

9. Write neatly so your teacher can read your work.

10. Listen up!

BE ON TIME.

DON'T TALK WHILE MS. BURT'S TALKING.

BODY LANGUAGE

When you're sitting in class, what do your actions say about your 'tude? Take a look at the pictures below. Now put yourself in the picture and think of what your body language might say to your teacher!

SURVIVAL TIP

Actions speak as loud as words! The actions of the kids in the pictures above shout "I DON'T CARE ABOUT WHAT YOU'RE TEACHING!" This is not a good message to be giving to your teacher. If you have a problem staying focused during class, see pages 20-21 for ways to help you tune in your teacher and tune out distractions.

How Do You Learn Best?

Everyone has a style of learning that works best for them. Whether it's one specific style or a combination, knowing what works for you will help you learn info and remember it. Answer the questions below to discover your special learning style. (And it's OK to have more than one answer!)

1. When putting something together, like a model airplane or a new toy, it's easiest for you if you . . .
   a. read the directions and look at the diagram.
   b. hear the directions read out loud.
   c. jump right in and start working with someone who knows how to do it.

2. When learning to play a new board game, it's easiest for you to . . .
   a. read the rules.
   b. hear the rules read out loud.
   c. start playing the game and learn as you go.

3. When making chocolate chip cookies, it's easiest for you to . . .
   a. read the recipe.
   b. hear the recipe read out loud.
   c. make cookies with someone and learn as you go.

4. When learning to play a new sport, it's easiest for you to learn by . . .
   a. watching the game being played.
   b. hearing the game explained.
   c. playing and learning as you go.

5. When making something new in art class, it's easiest for you if you . . .
   a. watch your teacher do it first.
   b. listen to your teacher explain it.
   c. start experimenting until you get it right.

6. When playing a video game for the first time, it's easiest for you if you . . .
   a. read the directions.
   b. listen as your friend reads them out loud.
   c. start playing and learn as you go.

ANSWER KEY

There is no right or wrong, only what works for you! Review the quiz and add up how many times you circled each letter. Then check below for the style—or styles—that help you learn best.

If you circled mostly A . . .

SEEING is believing. If you can get your eyes on the info—words, diagrams, movies, maps, pictures—your brain will process it. Turn to the Study Your Style section on pages 40–41 for tips on putting your study style to work.

If you circled mostly B . . .

HEARING helps you remember. From listening to class talks, to reading out loud, and to playing the radio, your brain tunes in when your ears do. Turn to the Study Your Style section on pages 40–41 for tips on putting your study style to work.

If you circled mostly C . . .

ACTION gets the info to sink in for you. Touching, moving, acting it out, writing, experimenting—for you, hands-on means your head's on, too! Turn to the Study Your Style section on pages 40–41 for tips on putting your study style to work.

LISTEN UP!

Did you know that most of the info you learn is presented orally by your teacher in class? That's why being a good listener is important to your success in school. Check out the listening tips below and learn some basic ways to concentrate better on what's being said.

FOCUS

Keep your eyes on the person who is talking. Focusing your eyes on the speaker will keep your mind focused, too.

SHAKE IT UP

Are you nodding off in class? Spacing out for long periods of time? Move a little. That's right, squirm in your seat. Roll your shoulders. Wiggle your fingers and toes. Give your head a little shake. Take a deep breath. Now that your body and brain are awake, tune back in to the speaker.

NOTE THIS

Take notes. It will make you a more active listener. Writing things down also reinforces what you hear and helps you to remember. For more note-taking tips, check out Take Note on pages 22-23.

ONE THING AT A TIME

It's very difficult to listen and do something else at the same time. So, when you're listening—just listen!

PICTURE IT!

Create a picture in your head of what's being said. If your teacher's reading a story out loud, imagine the characters in action.

PARTICIPATE

Make an effort to take part in class discussion. Staying involved will help you stay awake!

TUNE IN

Did you know that listening and hearing are not the same thing? Hearing simply means the words are entering your ears. Listening means that you are thinking about them and trying to understand and remember their meaning.

TAKE NOTE

Good note-taking is a skill that comes with practice. You don't want to have too little written down—or too much! Smart notes will make studying for tests a much simpler task. Here's a list of things to do to help you get the job done.

1. Write the date and subject at the top of the page. The date will serve as a good reference when you want to compare notes with friends. It'll also remind you of any days that you missed and need to get notes for.

2. Listen for the important stuff. You don't have time to write down everything your teacher says, so keep your ears open for the five Ws: Who, What, Where, When, and Why.

3. Shorten words and sentences. Save time by using abbreviations or make up your own shorthand. But be careful not to make your shorthand so short you can't figure out the original word you were abbreviating!

4. Put a question mark next to anything you didn't understand or didn't finish writing down. It'll help you remember to ask a friend or teacher later.

5. Underline, circle, or put a star next to anything the teacher repeats or emphasizes. That usually means it's Very Important Information!

6. Write down any questions your teacher asks. Questions are usually important and may show up on a test.

Missed Notes

If you're having trouble keeping up and are worried that you're missing important stuff, ask your teacher if you can bring a small tape recorder with you to record class. When you get home, listen to the tape while reviewing your notes to make sure you didn't miss anything. If you did, write it down.

Date and subject

October 17

O Alligators and How They Live

Write down important stuff!

Alligators are reptiles

How are alligators different from crocodiles?
1. lighter skin
2. tapered snout
3. less aggresive

Save time by shortening words and sentences, or by using abbreviations.

American alligators have tough, thick skin.

O Live in southeastern U.S.

Where? Rivers, marshes, swamps, lakes

? Alligators are carnivores — they eat

Use their tails to propel them thru water
— can swim up to 20 m.p.h.!
— use feet to paddle when going slow

Write down any questions your teacher asks.

Do alligators see the same as humans?

No — see black & white

O ★ Can live to 60!

Underline, circle, or star anything your teacher repeats.

Put a question mark by anything you didn't understand or didn't finish writing down.

Blooper!

"Sometimes my teacher calls on me even when I'm not raising my hand. If I get the answer wrong, the whole class laughs."

1. Kids who laugh at other kids when they answer a question wrong aren't very nice. People often laugh at others because they are feeling insecure. Perhaps they didn't know the answer either and are relieved they weren't in the hot seat—this time!

2. Remind yourself that even the best students answer questions wrong. That's why you go to school—to learn! If you had all the answers, you wouldn't need school!

3. Make sure you're prepared when you go to class. Did you do your homework? Did you review your notes?

Sometimes teachers call on students who aren't raising their hand because they don't participate on their own. To keep yourself out of a potentially embarrassing situation, take the initiative and raise your hand for questions when you do know the answer.

Blooper!

"I was walking to the front of the room to write on the chalkboard and I accidentally farted—loud enough for the whole class to hear!"

1. Horror of horrors—it just slipped out, and everyone knows it's you. Don't try to deny it, you're sure to create a bigger scene when all you really want to do is have people stop looking at you!

2. Politely say, "excuse me" like it's no big deal—because it's really not! (Everyone does it!)

3. Even though your face is burning and the class is howling, do your best to ignore them and focus on something else, like doing your problem at the board.

4. Sure, it's kind of gross, but it's natural. Remember that every kid in your class does it, too!

5. When class gets out, find some friends and let them comfort you. Hopefully, you'll be able to get a good laugh out of the silly situation and then forget about it. The rest of the class will, too.

Laugh At Yourself!

It makes you look confident even when you're not feeling confident. If you turn your mortifying moments into harmless jokes by laughing about them, people are less likely to make fun of you! After all, why would they bother to poke fun at you when you've already made fun of yourself? Remind yourself that what makes you cringe today will probably make you laugh in a couple of days— and turn it into a pretty funny story to tell, too!

THE KEY TO PUTTING TOGETHER A WINNING GROUP PROJECT? TEAMWORK!

Group projects are a lot like team sports. In order to succeed, everyone needs to play a part, try their hardest, and work together to achieve a common goal. Whether you're working on a science project with a couple of classmates, or writing a play for English class with a bigger group, here are some tips to get your team together and going strong!

TEAM CAPTAIN

It's a good idea to pick a group leader to keep everything together. The group leader should be responsible for writing down what everyone's job is, keeping notes, and marking important dates, like meetings and due dates, in a calendar. Being group leader doesn't mean being the boss!

HUDDLE!

Put your heads together and brainstorm until you agree on your goal. Brainstorming means coming up with a big list of ideas. It's important to be accepting of everyone's ideas and not make others feel bad if you don't like their suggestions. Once you have a list, narrow it down to the group's top two or three favorites and take a vote.

MAKE A GAME PLAN

Now that the group has a goal, follow these four steps for creating a plan to get it done!

To Do List

1) Make a list of all the things you need to do.

2) Rank the things in the order they should be completed.

3) Set deadlines for finishing each part of the project.

4) Divide up the work and give everyone a job to do.

HALF TIME

Meet as a group from time to time and check up on everyone's progress. Is everyone doing their part? Is the group still on schedule? Does a group member need help? These are all good things to go over.

PRACTICE

If your group is going to present something to the class, practice before you perform! It can only make the presentation better.

SCORE!

Every good athlete knows that winning takes teamwork. So does a good group project. A group is a powerful thing. Separately, each member can only carry so much weight, but together you can move mountains!

REFEREE, PLEASE!

What to Do When . . .

The Group Just Can't Agree

Making decisions as a group can be tough—because everyone has their own ideas! It's OK to disagree. The important thing is how you resolve it. Start by having a group discussion. Let each member give their opinion. Now can the group agree? If not, take a vote.

Group Members Don't Do Their Share

Is there a slacker in the pack? It's not fair if someone is relying on the rest of the group to do all the work. Have a group meeting and review what each person's job is. Ask if there's a reason that the person who isn't working hasn't done their share. Does he or she need help? If the person still isn't willing to pitch in, get a teacher's help. After all, that's what the teacher is there for!

SURVIVAL TIP

Everyone has their own opinions and ideas. In order for a group to work as a team, you have to be willing to compromise. Sometimes you have to bend your ideas to fit somebody else's. If everyone insisted on doing things their own way, nothing would get done!

GREAT PRESENTATIONS

Giving an oral report is like putting on a one-person show. It's your job to both inform and keep your audience interested. Follow these tips and put on a star performance!

PREPARE

Preparing an oral report is similar to preparing a written report. Unless the topic has been assigned, you should choose a subject that's interesting to you. What do you care about and want to learn more about? Follow your interests and you'll find your topic. For brainstorming tips, see page 69.

RESEARCH!

It's important to really know your subject. Use a variety of sources to find engaging and informative facts. For research tips, visit page 70.

PUT IT TOGETHER

Just like a written report, an oral report has three basic sections:

The Introduction introduces your subject. Hook your audience by catching their interest. Open with a thought-provoking question, interesting fact, true story, or personal experience that relates to your topic.

The Body is the main part of your report. If you were listening to a report on your subject, what would you want to know? Organize your outline around key points and focus on getting them across. Use visual aids, like posters, maps, slides, or pictures, to make your points and entertain your audience.

The Conclusion is where you summarize and get across your most important point. What do you want the audience to remember?

PEEK SHEET

It's hard to keep an audience interested if you stand in one place and just read. For some students, writing out the entire report word for word, then transferring the main points to note cards works best.

Others create an outline to guide them while speaking. Make sure you write BIG so you can read your notes at a glance, and use key words or short phrases instead of sentences.

MAKE EYE CONTACT

USE GESTURES

USE YOUR VOICE

PACE YOURSELF!

REHEARSE

Practicing is key to your success! Rehearse in front of a mirror, speak into a tape recorder, or just stand alone in your room. Time yourself to make sure your report is the right length. When you're comfortable with your presentation, practice on your family or a friend. Be open to any tips or helpful hints they offer.

REPORT

It's show time! Everyone is nervous before speaking in front of a group. Being prepared and comfortable with your info is the best way to combat nerves. Before you begin, take a deep breath. You may be nervous in the beginning, but once you start, you'll feel more comfortable.

These tips will help you give a polished presentation!

• Make eye contact. It helps the audience feel involved. If you're nervous, make eye contact with a friend. It's a lot better than staring at the floor or your notes!

• Use gestures. Your body language can help you make your points and keep the audience interested.

• Use your voice. Don't just babble on in the same tone, or mumble. Vary your tone and speak clearly.

• Pace yourself. When people get nervous, they tend to speed up their talking. If you find yourself hurrying, take a deep breath and slow down.

TROUBLE IN THE CLASSROOM

It's not always going to be smooth sailing. The school seas can get stormy, but don't panic! These tips will guide you into calmer waters.

POP QUIZ

IS YOUR TEACHER MEAN?

Put a T for true or an F for false by each statement. Then read on to see what your answers say about your teacher—and you!

MY TEACHER . . .

☐ 1. gives really hard tests.

☐ 2. picks on me in front of everyone.

☐ 3. assigns too much homework.

☐ 4. acts mad when I ask questions.

☐ 5. doesn't accept late homework.

TWO SIDES

Every story has two sides. There's your point of view and your teacher's. Sometimes it helps to look through different eyes!

MY TEACHER . . .

☐ **1. gives really hard tests.**

Does your teacher give hard tests because she's mean—or because she's trying to help you learn?

☐ **2. picks on me in front of everyone.**

Does your teacher pick on you because of the way you act? Check your own behavior. Do you talk while she's talking, yawn loudly, or stare out the window?

☐ **3. assigns too much homework.**

Is your teacher assigning homework to make the class miserable—or let you to practice what he's taught?

☐ **4. acts mad when i ask questions.**

Could your teacher be annoyed because you ask him to repeat things you would have heard if you'd been listening the first time?

☐ **5. doesn't accept late homework**

Rules are rules. Is your homework late for a good reason, like you were sick, or because you just didn't do it?

SURVIVAL TIP

If you've honestly looked at both sides of the situation and still feel that your teacher is mean, unkind, or unfair, talk to a parent or a counselor and let them help you resolve your teacher troubles.

NOT MORE TROUBLE?

THAT WAS A REALLY HARD TEST. COULD WE HAVE A REVIEW SESSION BEFORE THE NEXT ONE?

You want to talk to your teacher, but don't want to create more trouble for yourself? Know what to do and what to avoid! Make it your goal to have a conversation, not a confrontation. The following strategies will help you get what you want.

Be Polite.

Don't say

"That's not fair! Why did I get a C?"

Do say

"Excuse me, Miss Brown, could I please talk to you after class?"

Don't Blame.

Don't say

"Your tests are totally unfair!"

Do say

"That was a really hard test. Could we have a review session before the next one?"

Ask for Advice!

Don't say

"I don't get it!"

Do say

"Do you have any tips for getting this to sink in?"

CLASSMATE TROUBLES

From competition to copycats, check out these tips for dealing with the tough stuff.

HELP! When a friend distracts you in class by whispering in your ear and passing notes, or wanting to cheat

Write a quick note back asking your friend to "please stop!" or quietly shake your head "no." After class, talk to your friend and tell her how you feel. Real friends won't hold it against you. If they act mad, tell them you're sorry they're upset. But you don't have to apologize for not joining in or agreeing to cheat!

HELP! Competition in the classroom

Do you ever feel bummed out that your friend gets better grades than you even though you study harder? Or find yourself feeling jealous? It can be frustrating to study super hard and have your friend do better than you, even though he's barely cracked a book. The truth is, no matter who you are or what you're good at, there's almost always going to be someone who does just a little bit better. Accept it! Stop competing with your friend and don't ruin a good friendship. Next time you're feeling the competition, think about all the other things that you're good at instead.

BRAIN BUSTERS

YIKES!

Lots of kids feel pressure in the classroom. Some worry that they're stupid. Some worry that they're too smart. And some feel huge pressure to get good grades so they can please their parents. Read on for tips on what to do if one of those students is you!

HELP! "How come everyone understands but me?"

1. Everybody learns in different ways and at different speeds. Some people learn best when they hear the information, like a teacher speaking. Others learn best by reading, or seeing the information on a blackboard. And still others learn best by doing hands-on work, like science experiments. To find the study style that works best for you, turn to page 18. Whether it's one way or a combination, knowing what works best for you will help you take information in and remember it.

2. Just as there are different ways to learn, there are also different kinds of "smart." Grades are not really a measurement of how smart you are, but of how well you've learned the info given to you. There are many very smart students who don't get very good grades! Perhaps they didn't study. Or maybe they study really hard but get terrible test anxiety. Some students may do well on multiple-choice questions and draw a big blank when it comes to essay questions. The important thing about whatever grade you get is that you tried your hardest.

3. If you're really having trouble tackling a certain subject, get help! The important thing is that you understand the stuff. In school, ideas tend to build on themselves. If you don't understand early on, chances are your confusion will grow until you're completely lost! Before that happens, talk to a parent or teacher about getting some extra help, like a tutor to work with you one-on-one.

HELP! Feeling too much pressure to achieve?

Where is the pressure coming from? Are you putting pressure on yourself, or is the pressure coming from a parent or teacher? A little pressure can be a good motivator, but too much can make you so stressed out that you can't do anything well! Here are a few things to remember:

1. Parents and teachers want you to do your best. As a result, they may push you to try harder because they think that you're not working up to your ability. If you feel that you are, talk to your parent or teacher and let them know this. They really want (or should want) to help you, not hurt you!

2. If you're putting too much pressure on yourself, you need to remember this: Very few students get As in everything, and getting a B is certainly nothing to feel bad about! And believe it or not, the grade is not the most important thing, what you have learned is.

3. There's more to school than getting straight As! School is a place for finding out what you like to do and trying out new ideas. A successful student is one who works hard, has many interests, gets involved in activities, and has fun! So don't judge your success as a student only by your academic performance. There's so much more to it!

HELP! How to survive being the class "smarty pants."

Do people make fun of you because you're too smart? Even though the teasing hurts, you have to remember that they're probably jealous. After all, who doesn't want to get good grades? As long as you aren't a show-off, classmates shouldn't hold your high scores against you. Be happy for what you're good at! (And find more friends like yourself!)

Master That Test!

Teachers use tests to find out how well you've learned the stuff they've been teaching. Instead of thinking of tests as horrible obstacles to survive, think of them as challenges to master!

STUDY SMARTER

Even if you're a complete genius, you're going to have to prepare for tests and exams. There's no way around it. (If there were, we'd be happy to say so!) That means studying. So make the most of the situation and follow these strategies to get the job done right—and even have fun doing it!

DO YOU KNOW WHAT TO STUDY?

1. Start by reviewing your past tests and quizzes. Doing this will give you an idea of your teacher's test style. What kinds of questions does she ask? Where does she get most of her test questions? Are they from stuff taught in class, homework assignments, or readings? Use these clues to predict what might be on your next test.

2. Review your class notes. Highlight any info that the teacher emphasized or repeated, and any questions she asked. Highlight any of the Five Ws, too: who, what, where, when, and why. (For tips on taking great notes, turn to pages 22–23.)

3. Be sure to review past homework and reading assignments. You're likely to see much of this stuff resurface on the test. Highlight or star anything you need to study.

WHEN TO STUDY?

Give yourself plenty of time and start on the day the test is announced. Even though it's tempting to leave studying to the last minute, cramming isn't a good idea. If you stuff your brain too full of info without giving it time to sink in, you won't remember it for long! Break your studying into manageable bites and tackle some every day. Make the most of small chunks of time, too, like while you're riding the bus or waiting in the dentist's office. When you add up all those small chunks of time spent studying, they actually equal a pretty big chunk! The best way to memorize something is to see it again and again. When the test day comes, the info should be absorbed into your brain and easy to access!

WHO TO STUDY WITH?

Some students like to study alone. Others like to work with a classmate or in a study group. There's no right or wrong way, just what works for you. Here are some things to consider.

Two heads can sometimes be better than one. Studying with a friend, or in a study group, can be helpful because:

1. It will help you make—and stick to—a study schedule.

2. You can compare notes to see if you missed any info.

3. There's someone to explain what you don't understand.

4. You can learn new study techniques—maybe your study buddies have a trick you don't know.

5. You can quiz each other.

STUDY YOUR STYLE

Remember the learning style quiz you took on page 18? Here's your chance to put it to work. Look for the eye, ear, and hand symbols next to each idea to find your "study style."

 Making a study sheet is a good way to condense and organize important info. When reviewing the stuff, ask yourself questions and answer them, too.

 Flash cards. Using index cards, write a question or term on the front, and the answer on the back. Now quiz yourself. If you get the answer right, put the card aside. If you're wrong, put the card on the bottom of the pile and keep trying.

 Draw pictures. Some people remember things best when they can see a picture. Add art to your flash cards or study sheet to serve as reminders. During the test, you might not remember the answer at first, but seeing the picture in your head will jog your memory.

NIÑA   PINTA   SANTA MARIA

 Post it. Write important info on sticky notes and stick them in places you're sure to see them, like your closet door, bathroom mirror, or computer screen.

Read out loud from your notes, homework assignments, or any other stuff you need to learn. Hearing the info can help it stick in your mind.

 Record it. Record yourself reading your study sheet or flash cards. Then just hit play when you want to study. You can listen to your tape on the bus to school, sitting under a tree at recess, or right before the test!

 Make a video. Pretend you're a news anchor and have someone videotape you explaining the info as if you were actually delivering the news. Not only will making the video help you learn, but watching it will, too!

 Chart it. Make time lines, diagrams, graphs, or charts as another way to organize and view info.

 Make a sample test. Think of questions that your teacher might ask on the test and write them down. Use this test to test yourself, or swap sample tests with a study buddy and see how you do.

FLASHCARD FUN!

Try these games to liven up your study time. All you need is a pack of index cards, your study materials, and a study buddy or two.

CONCENTRATION

Come up with a list of 20 questions that could be on your test. Write each question on an index card. Now write the answers on another set of index cards. Shuffle them together and lay them out face down in rows of four. Just like in the card game, take turns picking a card, and then finding its match. Each player gets a chance—if that player misses, the next player goes. If a match is made, the player keeps the two cards, and goes again. At the end, the player with the most cards wins.

STUMPED!

Go through your study materials and come up with the ten hardest questions you can. Write the questions on the front and answers on the back of index cards. Have a partner do the same. Now take turns drawing a card from your opponent's pile and answering it. If you answer the question incorrectly, you take a letter from the word "stumped." The first player to spell S-T-U-M-P-E-D is out.

TIME OUT!

Don't let your study buddy become a distraction. If you're spending more time goofing off than you are studying, then it's best to part ways and plan to get together after the test.

STUDYING ALONE

Even if you study with a group or a friend, it's important to spend time studying on your own, too. Here's why:

1. You can study at your own pace.

2. You can study in your own way.

3. You can spend extra time reviewing your special study areas.

4. You have quiet and time to concentrate on the material.

SURVIVAL TIP

Whether studying in a group, or alone, the key to learning the material is to review it, practice it, say it out loud, and quiz yourself!

CHEAT SHEET!

TECHNIQUE	EXAMPLE
Acronyms Use the first letter of each word you're learning to make a sentence or a word that you can remember	**HOMES** (The Great Lakes: **H**uron, **O**ntario, **M**ichigan, **E**rie, **S**uperior)
Picture This . . . Form a picture in your mind of what you're trying to learn. Make it HUGE: Visualize it larger than life Make it MOVE: Have action in your image Make it MANY: Don't just visualize one, visualize lots!	Giraffes are herbivores.
Association Link words you're learning with something familiar.	**Rancid**—the smell of rotten milk
Rhyme Time Make up fun rhymes or simple songs.	"In 1492, Columbus sailed the ocean blue . . ."
Tell a Story Create a story where each word or idea you have to remember will cue the next idea you need to remember.	Christopher Columbus is a famous explorer. He is famous for his voyage of 1492. In 1492, he landed in America.

TEST DAY!

You've studied hard, had a good night's sleep, and eaten (a healthful) breakfast. You even had time to review your study sheet once more while waiting for the bus.

PANIC ATTACK!

Everyone feels nervous before a test. A little bit of nerves can actually motivate you.

Too much can be a problem, especially if it interferes with your ability to perform. Try these tricks for handling test anxiety:

1. Know your stuff! Cramming for a test is a poor way to learn and can cause test anxiety. The more confident you are that you know the material, the less anxious you'll feel about doing well.

2. Remind yourself that a test is only a test! It isn't a measure of your selfworth, just a measure of what you've learned.

3. Focus. Concentrate on answering the question, not on the grade you'll get.

4. Take deep breaths. Not only will breathing calm you, it also sends fresh oxygen to your brain to help it do its best!

Six Simple Ways to Improve Your Grade

These six tips can help you do better—and they have nothing to do with how much you know!

1. **Be Prepared.** Arrive early so you have a few minutes to collect your thoughts and get focused on the test ahead. Arrange sharpened pencils, scratch paper, erasers, a calculator, or a ruler on your desk.

2. **Follow Directions.** Listen to last-minute directions. They're likely to include important stuff you don't want to miss! When you get your test, read the directions twice and underline key words that explain what you should do. If you don't understand something, don't guess, ask your teacher.

3. **Make a Plan.** Take a moment to review the test to see how long it is and to plan how to best use your time. Don't waste time struggling with questions you can't answer. Begin with the questions you do know. Save the questions you don't know until the end.

4. **Brain Dump!** As soon as you get your test, jot down any stuff you're afraid of forgetting on the back, like important dates or tough equations.

5. **Don't Act Too Fast.** Read over all the answer choices before choosing. Even if you're sure you already spotted the right one, sometimes there's an even better one in the bunch!

6. **Check Your Work.** You've heard it a million times—review your work! Though you're sure you did it right the first time, you'll be amazed at what you may discover on a second read through. Use whatever time you have left at the end to check your test. After all, every point counts!

TEST TAKING TIPS

Use these strategies to help you with the toughest test questions!

TRUE OR FALSE? LUCKY GUESS!

1. Don't be fooled by a sentence that's only partly true. Watch for anything that will make the statement false.

2. Look out for words like "always" or "never." Because few things in life are "always" or "never," they can be clues that the answer is false.

3. Watch out for words that tend to make a statement true, like "usually," "probably," or "some."

4. If you really don't have a clue what the answer is, take a guess. Becase the answer is either true or false, you have a 50/50 chance of being right!

ESSAY QUESTIONS

1. Look for key words that tell you what's wanted in your essay. Underline them.

2. Organize your thoughts before you write. Jot down a brief outline on the back or side of the page to guide you.

3. State your main points.

4. Provide examples in your essay to back up your main points.

5. End your essay with a brief summary that emphasizes your main points.

What to do when you really don't know

Before you panic, take a moment to really think about the question. Is there any part of it you can answer? Any dates that relate? Places? People? Get something down that shows your teacher you have some understanding and knowledge of the info. Don't give up!

MULTIPLE CHOICE

1. Before looking at the choices, read the question and answer it in your head. Sometimes reading the choices first can cause you to jumble up the facts in your mind.

2. Read all your choices before answering. Even if you're sure the first answer is it, read on, there could be a better answer.

3. If you don't know the answer, use the process of elimination. Narrow your choices down to two and make a guess.

4. When two very similar answers appear, there's a good chance that one of them is the correct choice. Teachers often disguise the right answer by giving another that is confusingly similar!

SURVIVAL TIP

If you're down to a couple of choices, choose the answer that's longer and more descriptive. Teachers often give lots of description to help you identify the truth.

TICK-TOCK—TIME'S ALMOST UP!

You only have seven minutes left! What do you do when you have too much to do? Stop! Quickly scan your test and ask yourself these questions:

1. What sections are worth the most points?

2. What questions do I know the answers to?

3. How long will each section take me?

Try to earn the most points in the time you have left. Answer the questions that you know the answers to and that won't take too long. If you're struggling with an essay question that's worth 20 points, and the true/false section (which is easier for you) is worth the same, give up on the essay and switch to true/false.

Go for partial credit. Teachers will often give some credit if you show that you know the stuff. Work out the first part of a math equation, or jot down any info that may relate to your essay topic.

WHEN YOU GET YOUR TEST BACK

Don't just look at the grade and stuff your test in your knapsack. Go over what you got wrong so you can learn from your mistakes. When reviewing your test, ask yourself: Did I follow the directions? Is there a pattern to my mistakes? Did I make careless errors that I could have caught if I had reread my work? Did I run out of time?

Pay attention to the areas you need to brush up on and make sure you understand any questions you got wrong, so you can learn that material for next time. If necessary, set up a meeting to go over your test with your teacher.

Master Friends, Foes, and After-School Stuff

There's more to school than homework, classes, tests, and grades. School is also about meeting people, making friends, and discovering things you like to do. From sports teams to school plays, there are plenty of opportunities for getting involved—and meeting cool people along the way. But just like anything, the social side of school can have some bumps in its path. From peer pressure to bullies, this section is packed with tips to help you master the social stuff!

GET INVOLVED

Participating is school activities is a great way to meet people with the same interests as you. It's also how you discover things that you like to do and are good at. From after-school clubs to student government, every school offers something. What do you like to do? Here are some ideas to get you thinking.

- If you're interested in acting, try out for the school play.
- If you're interested in singing, think about joining the chorus.
- If you love sports, try out for a sports team.

- If you like to write, work on the school newspaper.
- If you like to take pictures, join the yearbook staff.
- If you're interested in making a difference, run for a class office.

HELP! WHEN YOU DON'T GET CHOSEN

Whether it's for the play, the soccer team, or class president, the disappointment of not being picked can be huge. These tips will help you master the situation:

1. Any time you have to try out for something, there's a chance you're not going to be selected. There can be a lot of competition and more than one person can be right for the part or position. Trying out or being elected is part of the process.

2. Take a little time to be by yourself. Collect your thoughts and composure.

3. You certainly don't want to seem like a poor sport. Congratulate friends and classmates who did get selected.

4. Ask for suggestions on what you can do to improve your chances for when you try out next time.

5. Polish your skills. Do what you can to better your chances for getting a spot in the future.

The best way to make it is to try again!

Bright Idea

START YOUR OWN CLUB!

Clubs are a great way to get together with old friends and make new ones. They're also a great way to spend time doing something you enjoy. Almost anything you like to do can make a great club. Follow these simple steps to start your own!

JOIN The DOGWALKERS CLUB!

IF YOU LOVE DOGS, COME TO OUR FIRST MEETING!

MONDAY DECEMBER 5 at 3:00 in the cafeteria

BRING FRIENDS!

Step 1: Club Ideas

When choosing your club's theme, think about things you'd like to learn about or spend time doing. Write down a list of all your ideas and choose your favorite.

Step 2: Finding New Members

In addition to your buds, look for additional members outside your circle of friends. Make posters or fliers announcing your new club and the time, place, and date of the first meeting. Post them on bulletin boards at school and pass them out at lunch.

Step 3: The First Meeting

If you plan on holding meetings at school, talk with your teacher about a good place to do so, and get permission. Other possible meeting places are someone's house or the public library. For most clubs, meeting once a week or every other week is enough. Sometimes, once a month will do.

Step 4: Club Notes and Other Important Info

Keep important stuff in a special club notebook. Make a list of things you want to talk about at each meeting. Use the notebook to take notes, record votes, and write down each member's name and phone number.

Step 5: A Job for All

Put everyone's talents to work. Make a list of jobs, like president, vice president, secretary, or snack planner, and a list of their responsibilities. Have members volunteer, or hold an election and take a vote.

Step 6: Group Gripes

Let everyone have a say, and if the group can't agree, take a vote. You can raise your hands, or take a secret vote and write your decision on pieces of paper and have someone count them. If there's a tie, flip a coin and let that be the final decision.

Do It!

Here are some ideas to help you start your own club!

1. **Animal Lovers' Club:** Plan fun field trips to zoos, aquariums, and wildlife museums.

2. **Drama Club:** Write and put on your own plays.

3. **Camping Club:** Learn survival tricks, how to put up tents, and eat s'mores.

4. **Save the Environment Club:** Plant trees, pick up litter, and spread the word on recycling.

5. **Charity Club:** Work together to raise money and donate it to a favorite charity—or charities.

6. **Bike Club:** Plan fun bike rides to take as a group.

7. **Sports Club:** Play your favorite sport and go to games.

8. **Book Club:** Read your favorite books and talk about them.

9. **Hobby Club:** Coin collecting, drawing, cooking—any hobby will make a great club.

Cliques and Peer Pressure

There's nothing wrong with having a group of friends to hang out with. The important thing is not to let the group persuade you to lose sight of what's right. What would you do if caught in any of these situations?

My friends and I have a special table in the lunchroom that we eat at every day. When the new boy asked if he could sit with us, everyone said no, so he sat alone. I wanted to join him, but I knew my friends would make fun of me.

There's a girl in my class who my friends tease. It makes me feel bad, but I go along with the group because I don t want them to pick on me instead.

My friends think it's fun to steal candy from the store down the street. I don't like doing it, but they said if I didn't, I couldn't hang out with them anymore.

None of the popular kids at my school want to try out for the talent show. I want to, but I'm afraid if I do they'll think I'm a loser and I won't be popular anymore.

BE A LEADER, NOT A FOLLOWER!

If the group is doing stuff that you know is wrong or cruel, then it's time to clique off!

Don't let the power of any group control you. If that little voice inside your head is saying that it's wrong, it probably is. The only person responsible for your actions is you! So be true to yourself. Listen to your head. Follow your heart. Don't be afraid to tell others you don't agree with them. If they get mad, say you're sorry that your actions upset them, but you don't have to apologize for not joining in. Your real friends will respect you!

DEALING WITH BULLIES

Bullies pick on others to make themselves feel powerful and important. Some are just looking for attention. Getting a reaction out of you can make bullies feel like they have the power they want. Don't let bullies get the best of you!

Here are some things to try if you're being picked on.

1. Act brave and ignore the bully. It's no fun to pick on someone if they don't react. Acting like you don't care may be enough to get the bully to back down. Eventually, the bully will get bored and move on.

2. Stand up for yourself. Simply say "please stop" and walk away.

PLEASE STOP

3. Agree with the bully's insults. It's no fun to tease someone who isn't bothered by it.

4. Tell an adult. If the bullying is more than you can handle, or if the bully is physically hurting you, talk to a teacher, principal, or parent immediately. They can all help stop bullying.

HELP! "A GIRL IN MY CLASS STARTED A RUMOR ABOUT ME. NOW EVERYONE LAUGHS AT ME WHEN I WALK DOWN THE HALL."

1. No matter what you say or do, some people are going to believe the rumor. Since you can't make everyone believe you, make it your goal to lessen the damage.

2. When you hear the rumor, don't freak, play it cool. If you overreact, people will think you actually do have something to hide. If you don't make a big deal out of it, others usually won't either.

3. Laugh it off and make a point of asking "Why would someone go to so much trouble to spread a lie?" This makes the person who started the rumor look like the foolish one!

4. Control the spread of the rumor by spreading it yourself. "Have you heard what's being said about me? What a joke!"

5. Confront the person who started the rumor. It's best to do this when you're calm and in private. Ask the person why she's spreading a lie about you and ask her to stop.

SURVIVAL TIP

Getting along with your classmates won't always be easy. Chances are you won't like everyone, and some kids won't like you, either. Being accepted by others is what most kids want. But understanding that others may not always like you is the first step to being happy and comfortable with yourself. Be true to yourself—and true friends will follow.

Master Your Time!

Once school is out there are papers to write, math assignments to finish, and reading to tackle. Use these tips and have time leftover for fun.

Too Much to Do? Don't Bite Off More Than You Can Chew!

Do you have a problem balancing friends, homework, family, school, hobbies, sports, and all the other important parts of your day? Lots of kids do because they overcommit. They fill up their schedule with too many after-school activities. The big question is how much can you really do? Planning is the key to making a busy schedule work. To make the best use of your time, create an after-school schedule. It will help you figure out what you have time for and what you don't!

CHECK POINT

BEFORE YOU TAKE OFF AT THE END OF THE DAY

Make sure you:

- check your assignment book so you know what you need to bring home
- pack up all of the books you'll need overnight

Bright Idea

MAKE AN AFTER-SCHOOL SCHEDULE

1. Start by filling in all the things you have to do like sports practice, music lessons, dinner, chores, and sleeping.

2. Now block out time for homework.

3. And finally—free time! This includes stuff like watching TV, reading just for fun, and hanging out with your family and friends.

Time	M	T	W	T	F
3:00-4:00	Soccer Practice	Piano Practice	Soccer Practice	Student Council	Soccer Practice
4:00-5:00	Chores	Free	Piano Practice	Piano Lesson	Free
5:00-6:00	Dinner				
6:00-8:00	Homework				
8:00-9:00	Free Time!				
9:30	Bedtime				

THE BIG QUESTION

Review your schedule and ask yourself: Is my schedule balanced? Remember, you want to have a schedule that you can both manage and enjoy! Along with all your activities, is there enough free time? What about family time? And of course, homework? If you feel worried that you've bitten off too much, talk with your parent or teacher. See if they can help you reorganize your schedule or help you figure out something to drop.

HOMEWORK!

Everybody who goes to school does homework. Teachers give homework so you can practice new skills and review others—not as torture! You can't escape homework, hide from it, or pretend it doesn't exist. What's the only way to make homework disappear? Do it!

TIME CHECK

Check the after-school schedule you made on page 61. Do your homework in the time slots you selected, and save the fun for when you're done.

Don't do homework when . . .

1. you're hungry.

2. you're sleepy.

3. you can't concentrate.

Don't waste time wishing you were doing something else. Make sure you have a snack, take a quick nap if you need to, and grab short fifteen-minute breaks to restore your concentration. Then get back to work!

PLACES, PLEASE

Have a special place where you do your homework every day. That way, when you sit down, your brain will automatically click into study mode. Go back to page 11 for tips on creating a study space that works for you!

HARDEST FIRST

Tackle the tough stuff first, while your mind is still fresh. Save the easier assignments for later.

SMART SNACKS

Before you sit down to study, energize your brain by eating a healthful snack. Skip the sugary stuff. It may give you a burst at first, but you will quickly lose energy. Try these power boosts instead!

DIP IT!

- Dip granola bars into yogurt.
- Dip apple slices into peanut (or cashew or almond) butter.
- Dip carrots and celery into your favorite salad dressing.

TORTILLA TOPPERS

Spread the following combos on a tortilla, roll it up, and enjoy!

- Peanut butter and jelly topped with bananas
- Spaghetti sauce topped with parmesan cheese

FROZEN FRUITS

- Insert a popsicle stick into a peeled banana. Put the banana on a plate and freeze it for at least one hour. For a tasty twist before you freeze the banana, drizzle it with honey and sprinkle it with shredded coconut, granola, or chopped nuts.
- Put a bunch of grapes in the freezer for at least one hour, then pop them in your mouth and enjoy.

BREAK IT UP!

Take big assignments and split them into manageable chunks. Look at your calendar and work back from the due date. Figure out how much you have to do each day to be finished by that date. Do it!

MINUTES MATTER

Do some homework while you're riding on the bus, waiting to be picked up from play practice, or in the dentist's waiting room. Lots of small chunks of time put together equal a big chunk of time! Make the most of it to get some homework done.

INTERMISSION

If you find yourself spacing out and squirming in your chair, take a short break. What's the point of sitting at your desk watching the time tick by and doing nothing? Set a break time, like fifteen minutes. Then get up and stretch, walk the dog, or go for a bike ride. When you come back to your homework, your mind should be refreshed and ready to go.

REWARD YOURSELF!

Your homework is done and you deserve a reward! What fun things are you going to do when you finish your homework? Watch your favorite TV show? Go on a bike ride? Play with the dog? Call your best friend? With the work out of the way, your path is clear for play. Enjoy!

HOMEWORK HURDLES

The following problems are no excuse for not getting your homework done. Don't let them stop you!

HURDLE: I HAVE TOO MUCH HOMEWORK!

If you're having a problem finishing, take an honest look at your homework habits. Are you struggling with a certain subject and it takes extra long to complete the work? Are you distracted by the TV in the background? Do you have too many after-school activities? Are you putting off big assignments until the last minute? The key to getting it done is to plan your time and use it wisely. Make and stick to your homework schedule. (See page 61 to make one.) Also set aside a certain amount of time to spend on each task, like 30 minutes. Then spend that time really focusing on the subject. If the work is really too hard, get help from a parent or teacher. Or ask for a tutor's help.

HURDLE: I LEFT THE BOOK I NEED AT SCHOOL

If it's too late to go back to school, call a classmate and see if he can help you out. If he's finished with the book, maybe you can borrow it—if not for the evening, perhaps long enough to get the info you need copied on a copy machine. But the best solution is prevention! Don't rely on your memory when packing up to go home. Take the time to check your assignment book before you leave school. Check each item off as you put it in your bag to take home.

HURDLE: I DIDN'T GET THE ASSIGNMENT BECAUSE I WAS OUT SICK

Being sick isn't going to get you out of homework! Most teachers consider it your responsibility to find out what you missed and make up the work once you're well. Call a classmate to find out what you missed. Have a sibling or friend bring home any books or handouts you may need.

HURDLE: I'M STUCK!

Don't give up! Check your class notes for clues, and review your readings. If you're still stuck, ask for help. Perhaps a parent or sibling can guide you. If not, call a classmate. Or use a homework helper Web site, like: Discoveryschool.com (http://school.discovery.com/students) or Ask Jeeves® Kids (http://www.ajkids.com)

HELP! THE DOG ATE MY HOMEWORK

1. Dogs don't eat homework and teachers know it! Whether you have a good reason for not doing your homework, like you were sick, or you have no good reason, like you were watching TV, your best bet is to tell your teacher the truth. Telling the truth doesn't get you off—it just helps you save face! If there's a good reason why you didn't do it, have a parent write a note explaining the situation.

2. If you don't have a good reason for not getting it done, take a look at your attitude. It's almost impossible to be successful at school if you don't do your homework. Everyone gets behind sometimes, but the key is to get yourself out of the hole before you're in too deep!

READING

Many students open their books, read until they finish, and consider the assignment done. But just because your eyes soaked up the words doesn't mean your brain did! Find out how to get your reading to sink in and stick.

1. Preview

Scan the material before you start reading. How long is it? What's it about? Read the headings. Knowing what the reading is about before you start will prepare you for what you're going to learn.

2. Get a Clue

Textbooks often have questions at the end of each chapter. Reviewing them before you start reading will alert you to the really important stuff.

3. Baby Bites

How long can you read and truly concentrate? If you have a long reading assignment, break it into pieces and read just a bit at a time.

4. Be Active!

Use a highlighter to underline important stuff. Put a star by anything super important and a question mark by anything you don't understand. If the book isn't yours, take notes on a piece of paper. Write down important stuff and any questions you may have. Or mark important pages with sticky notes that you can remove. Make brief notes on the stickies to remind yourself why you marked the page.

5. The End

Once you've finished the reading, test yourself by using your own words to summarize what the reading was about. If you can't, you better read it again!

WRITING

Book reports, research papers, essays—writing assignments can have many purposes, but the basics are the same. Don't let the thought of turning your ideas into sentences, and your sentences into great papers intimidate you. Follow a few simple steps, and your paper will almost write itself!

SIX STEPS TO A GREAT PAPER

To make the job more manageable, break the project into steps. Then focus on accomplishing one step at a time.

STEP 1: SELECT A TOPIC

In some cases, your teacher will assign a topic. Other times you'll be free to choose. Having to choose a topic can make getting started even harder. Here's the good news—you can write about your own interests! To help you come up with ideas, brainstorm. To get started, jot down:

1. Your favorite things to do
2. Things you'd like to learn about
3. Places you'd like to see
4. Famous people you'd like to meet
5. A moment in history you'd like to experience

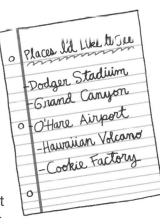

Review your list for a topic that fits the requirements. It may not be obvious at first, but one of your ideas can probably be molded to fit the assignment.

STEP 2: RESEARCH

Now that you have your topic, it's time to start gathering the facts. Don't just rely on one source for all your info—use a variety of sources. Here are some good places to look:

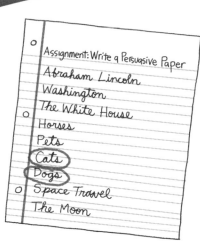

Assignment: Write a Persuasive Paper
Abraham Lincoln
Washington
The White House
Horses
Pets
Cats
Dogs
Space Travel
The Moon

Library: Ask a librarian to help you get started in your search. From finding newspaper archives to book titles, the librarian can give you lots of good tips!

Books: Always a good reliable source of info.

Encyclopedias: Great for finding general stuff and getting an overview of your subject.

Videos and DVDs: Packed with info and fun to watch. Make sure to take good notes!

Museums: If there's one in your area, check to see if there are any specific exhibits that relate to your topic.

Magazines & Newspaper Archives: Offer specific stories and true events.

Interviews: Put a list of questions together and talk to a pro.

Internet: Type your subject into a search engine and see what pops up. Online encyclopedias are also a good and reliable source of info. Print out any helpful stuff you may want to use. Make sure your Internet source is a reliable one—use stuff offered by established organizations instead of unknown individuals.

SURVIVAL TIP

Keep a list of all the sources you use. Write down the title, author, and publisher. That way if anyone asks where you got something, or if you have to go back to the source, you'll have it.

DON'T PROCRASTINATE!

It's easy to put off papers until right before they're due. Don't let time creep up on you! Not only will the quality of your paper suffer, but having to pack lots of work into a short period of time can make the experience miserable. Start the day your teacher gives the assignment. Use a calendar to help you organize your time. Work back from the due date and figure out how long it will take you to complete each of the following six steps. Stick to your time line!

STEP 3: ORGANIZE YOUR IDEAS

Now that you've gathered your facts, create a simple outline of your paper. The writing process will be much easier if you organize your ideas before you start! Here's what you do:

1. Write your topic at the top of the page.

2. Each paragraph in your paper gets a Roman numeral. Next to each Roman numeral, write the main point of the paragraph.

3. Under each paragraph, list the facts that support the main idea. Label these with letters.

4. Give examples to support each fact. Label these with regular numbers.

> Why Cats Make Great Pets
>
> I. Dogs are not the only pets people enjoy
>
>   A. For many people, a cat is their best friend
>
>   B. Despite what dog lovers believe, cats make great house pets
>
> II. People enjoy the companionship of cats
>
>   A. Cats are affectionate and playful
>
>   1. like to snuggle
>
>   2. like to chase balls
>
>   B. Cats are civilized and can be trained

STEP 4: WRITE YOUR INTRODUCTORY PARAGRAPH

The intro paragraph is the first one of your paper. It introduces the main idea of your essay and should capture the reader's interest. The main idea of the paper is stated in a single sentence. All the info you present in your paper will back up and support this one idea. Look at your outline and decide what the main point you will be making is. Your main idea should be the last sentence of the intro paragraph.

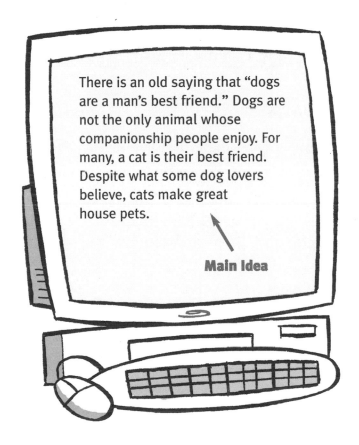

There is an old saying that "dogs are a man's best friend." Dogs are not the only animal whose companionship people enjoy. For many, a cat is their best friend. Despite what some dog lovers believe, cats make great house pets.

Main Idea

STEP 5: SUPPORTING PARAGRAPHS

Supporting paragraphs make up the main body of your essay. Each supporting paragraph should help you prove the point you're making. Like all good paragraphs, supporting paragraphs should have sentences that give facts, details, and examples backing up the main sentence.

Cats are affectionate. They like to snuggle and be scratched behind the ears. They will curl up in your lap and take a nap. They also purr when you pet them. Who can resist a purring cat?

Cats are also playful. They like to chase balls, bells, and hit at anything dangling on a string. They really like playing with their owners.

STEP 6: THE CONCLUSION

The conclusion is the last paragraph of your essay. It should summarize or restate the main points, or briefly describe your feelings about the topic.

Cats are low maintenance, civilized companions. They are affectionate, playful, and clean. They also make very little noise and don't bark. In many ways, cats are ideal house pets.

Rereading and Revising

One of the most important things you can do to improve your grade is to take the time to carefully read your paper before you turn it in. Look at your paragraphs and ask yourself:

1. Do I have a main idea?

2. Does my paper support my main idea?

3. Are my sentences clearly written? Do they flow smoothly?

Keep your eyes open for ways to improve your paper. The first draft is rarely good enough to turn in. Once you get the words down, you're likely to find a bunch of ways to make your paper even better. That's called revising, and revising is an important part of the writing process. It's what turns a good paper into a great paper!

Presentation

Even papers make a first impression! Make sure yours makes a good one by using this checklist.

- [ ] Have you created a title page with your name, date, class, and paper title?
- [ ] Have you spell checked and grammar checked? (The computer won't catch every error, but it might catch errors you've missed.)
- [ ] Have you numbered the pages?
- [ ] Did you double space your lines?
- [ ] Is your work printed on clean, white paper?
- [ ] Is your paper in a report cover or stapled together?

When typing your paper on a computer, remember to:

1. Save your work often so it doesn't get lost!

2. Back up your work! Print out drafts as you go along and save your info on a disk.

Why Cats Make Great Pets
Amanda Zimmer
English   December 1

QUICK TIP PUNCTUATION GUIDE

Stumped? Use this basic guide to solve your punctuation problems!

Punctuation Mark	Use	Example
?	Use a question mark at the end of a sentence to show a direct question	What is your favorite food?
!	Use an exclamation point to show excitement or surprise	I love hot dogs!
.	Use a period to show the end of a sentence.	Hot dogs are my favorite food.
,	Use a comma to show a pause in a sentence. Use a comma for listing three or more different things. Use commas around clauses that add extra information to a sentence.	Because Sammy loves hot dogs, his mom is planning to serve them at the party. Sammy's mom served hot dogs, potato chips, and cake. Sammy's mom, who was the host of the party, makes great hot dogs.
" "	Use quotation marks when using somebody else's words. Use quotation marks to show that someone is speaking.	When I asked Sammy what his favorite food is, he answered, "I love hot dogs!" "I love hot dogs," said Sammy.

WORDS TO WATCH OUT FOR!

These commonly confused words are the kind of mistakes spell check can't detect! Can you?

When to use	Definition	Example
it's, its	*It's* is the short form of "it is." *Its* is a pronoun that shows ownership or possession.	**It's** in the car. That car has a mind of **its** own.
than, then	Than means in "comparison with." Then means "next."	He is stronger **than** me. First I went to the candy store, and **then** I went to the library.
their, there, they're	Their is a form of "they" that shows ownership. There describes where something is. They're is the short form of "they are."	**Their** tree house is so cool. The car keys are over **there**. **They're** going to let me go home early.
to, too	To means "in the direction of." Too means "also or besides." Too can also mean excess.	My family went **to** the airport. My friend came along to the airport, **too.** He ate **too** much candy during the movie.
your, you're	Your is a form of "you" that shows ownership. You're is the short form of "you are."	**Your** dog is cute. **You're** so lucky to have such a cute dog.

SPELLING BEE CHALLENGE

Can you correctly spell these frequently misspelled words? They are all misspelled here. Buzz on over to the answer key to see how you did!

1. welcom
2. bigest
3. acomplish
4. beleve
5. desert (like ice cream)
6. truely
7. embaras
8. goverment
9. grammer
10. exsided
11. geting
12. begining
13. particuler
14. tomatos
15. potatos
16. solveing
17. recomend
18. scarey
19. succes
20. spagetti

AND FINALLY

Before Going to Bed

Pack up everything you need for school the next day, like:

- ✓ finished homework
- ✓ books
- ✓ plenty of paper and sharpened pencils or pens
- ✓ lunch or lunch money
- ✓ signed permission slip, if you have one
- ✓ sneakers or gym clothes

ANSWER KEY

1. welcome	11. getting
2. biggest	12. beginning
3. accomplish	13. particular
4. believe	14. tomatoes
5. dessert	15. potatoes
6. truly	16. solving
7. embarrass	17. recommend
8. government	18. scary
9. grammar	19. success
10. excited	20. spaghetti

SECRETS OF MASTER STUDENTS

Anyone can be successful at school and have fun doing it! As you learned by reading this book, you don't have to be a genius, but you do have to be dedicated—you have to try! To sum it all up:

- Have a winning attitude and plan to succeed!
- Have a plan and work to achieve it.
- Don't bite off more than you can chew. Make sure you have a balanced schedule that you can manage and enjoy.
- Don't procrastinate. Just do it!
- Take care of yourself. Get a good night's sleep so you can be sharp. Fuel your body and brain with healthy foods.
- Participate. From class discussions to group projects, being involved helps you learn.
- Take part in extracurricular activities. School isn't just about classes and grades. It's also about trying new things, discovering what you're good at, and having fun!
- Have school spirit! Give it your all!

And by coming to the end of this book, you now know how to succeed in the school universe! The rest is up to you. Armed with this book, the techniques you learned while reading, and your super attitude, you now have the confidence to master school and have fun, too!